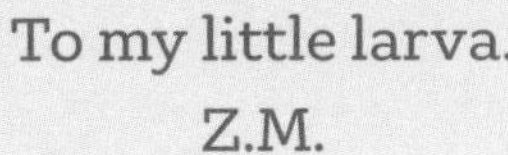

To my little larva.
Z.M.

For darling Charlie and Alf.
And for my First Friday ants, of course.
J.D.

First published in 2024 by
Museums Victoria Publishing

11 Nicholson Street
Carlton, Victoria 3053, Australia
publications@museum.vic.gov.au

www.museumsvictoria.com.au

Many thanks to Museums Victoria Research Institute entomologists Ken Walker and Simon Hinkley, whose expertise and guidance were invaluable during the making of this book.

A catalogue record for this book is available from the National Library of Australia.

ISBN 9781921833700

Design by Julia Donkersley
Production by Sasha Beekman
Printed in China by RR Donnelley Asia Printing Solutions, Ltd.

1 3 5 7 9 10 8 6 4 2

Museums Victoria acknowledges the Wurundjeri Woi Wurrung and Boon Wurrung peoples of the eastern Kulin Nations where we work, and First Peoples language groups and communities across Victoria and Australia. Our organisation, in partnership with the First Peoples of Victoria, is working to place First Peoples living cultures and histories at the core of our practice.

This book has been created by Museums Victoria, Australia's largest public museum organisation. Our venues include Melbourne Museum, Scienceworks, Immigration Museum and Royal Exhibition Building. Proceeds from the sale of this book support Museums Victoria's collections and ongoing research.

Zoe Meagher Julia Darling

An Ant's Guide to BEING AN ANT

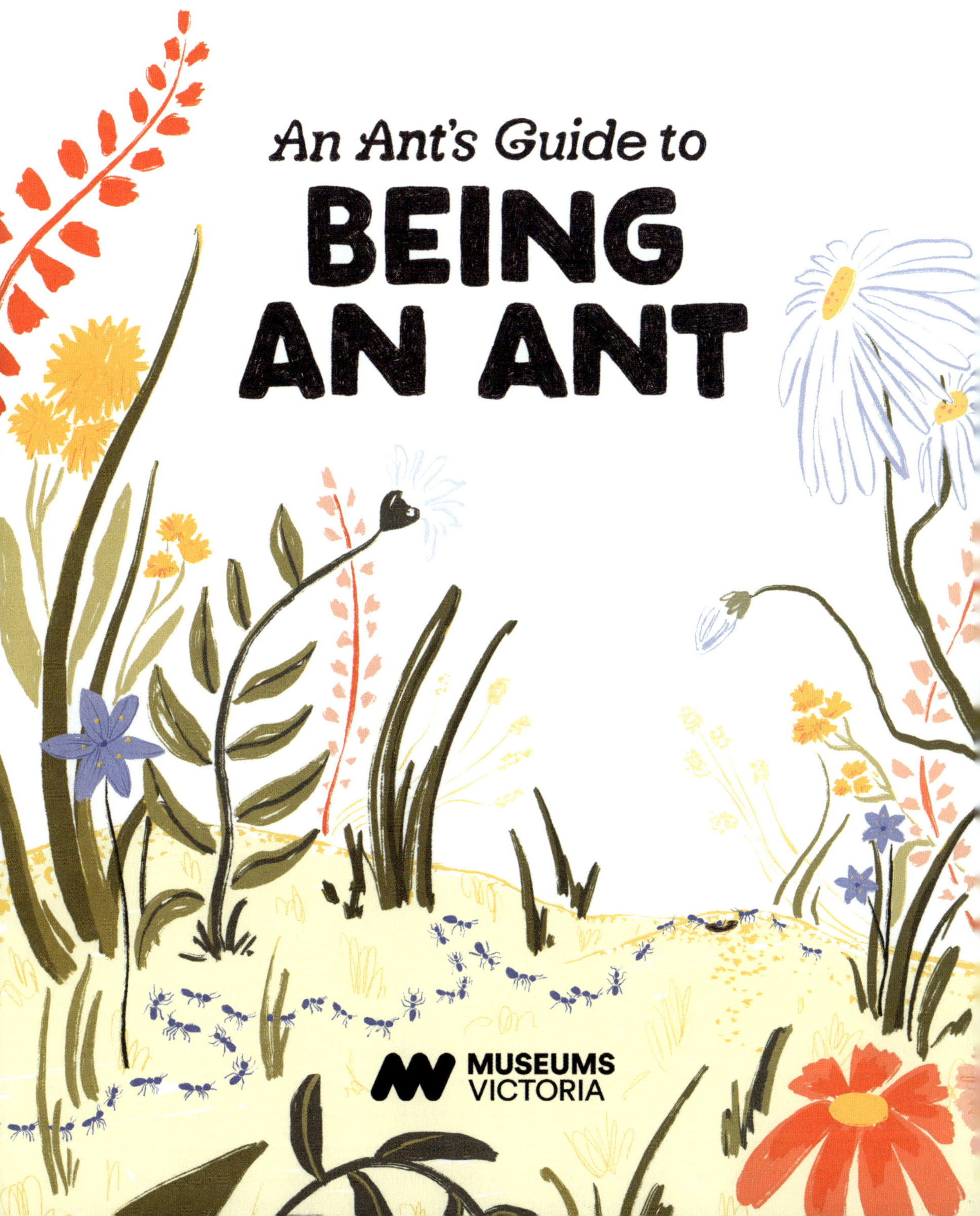

MUSEUMS VICTORIA

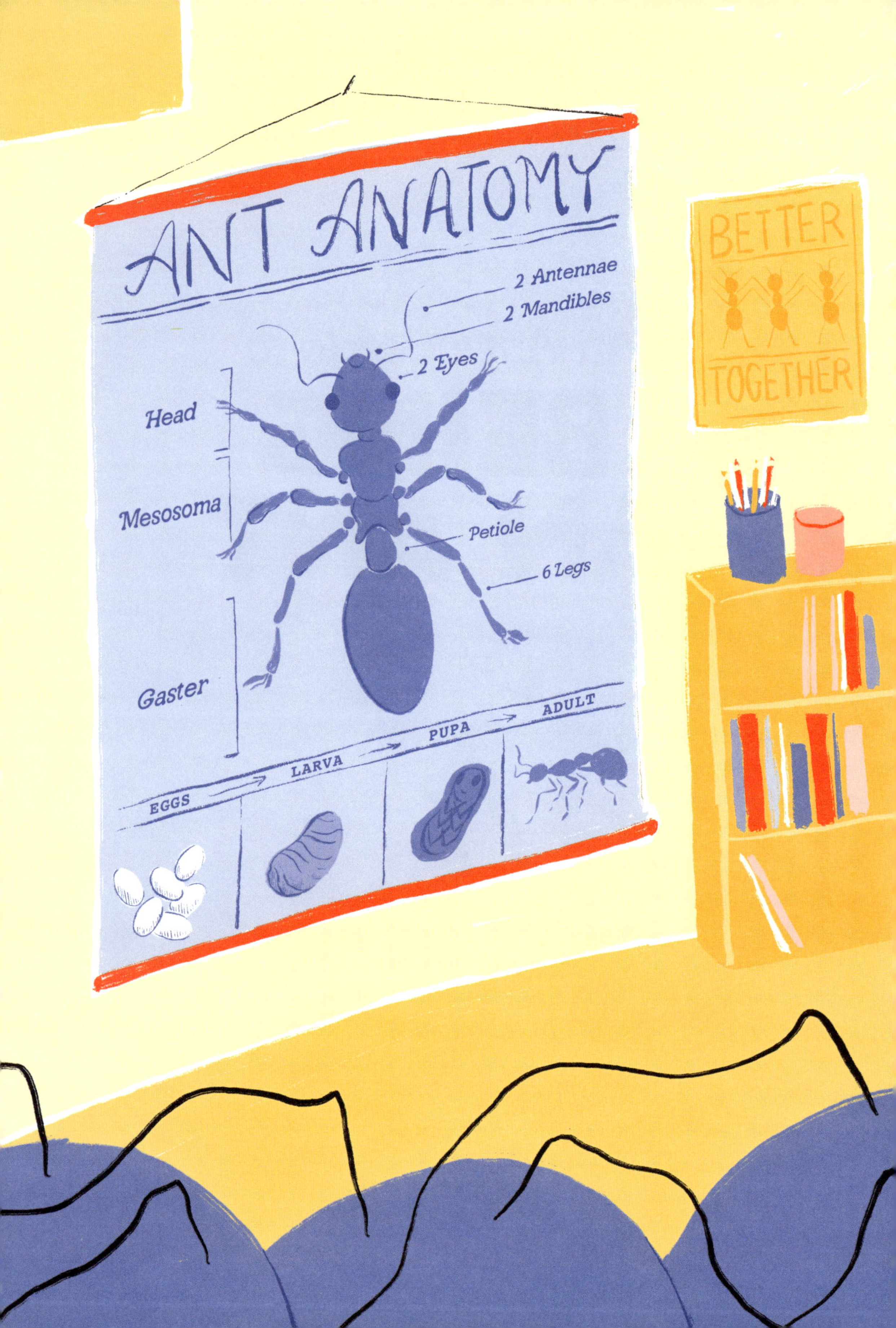
ANT ANATOMY
2 Antennae
2 Mandibles
2 Eyes
Head
Mesosoma
Petiole
6 Legs
Gaster
EGGS
LARVA
PUPA
ADULT
BETTER
TOGETHER

RULE #1.

This book is for ants.
If you are not an ant,
DO NOT READ this book.

RULE #2.

If you are a worker ant
(no wings, small, can't lay eggs)
then you have to WORK.
Your job is whatever
your family (colony) needs:

Digging new
rooms in the nest.

Going outside
to get food.

Looking after baby sisters.

RULE #3.

If you're a queen (wings*, big, lays heaps and heaps of eggs), your job is EGGS. 400 a year is passable …

*At first. Then the wings fall off.

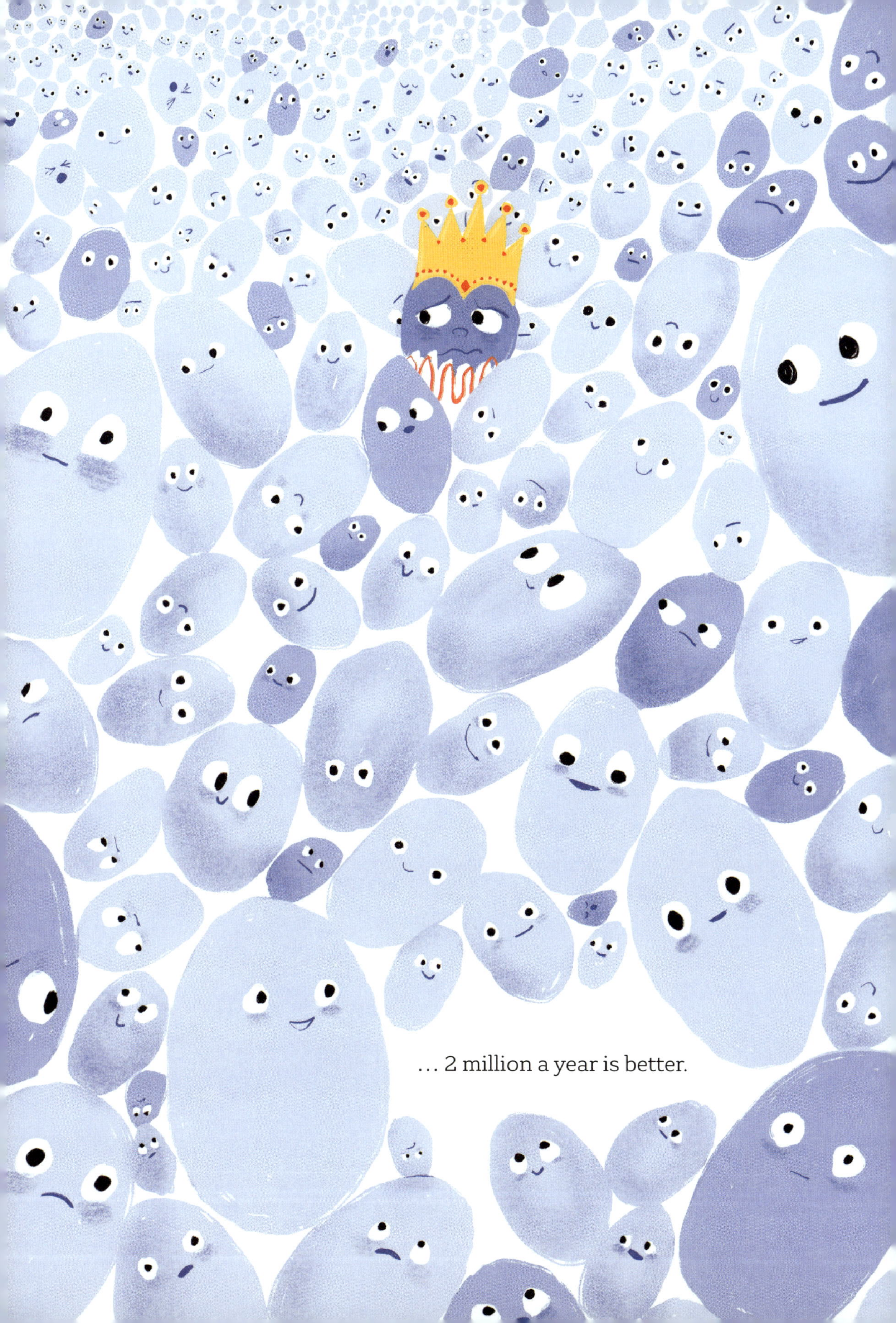

… 2 million a year is better.

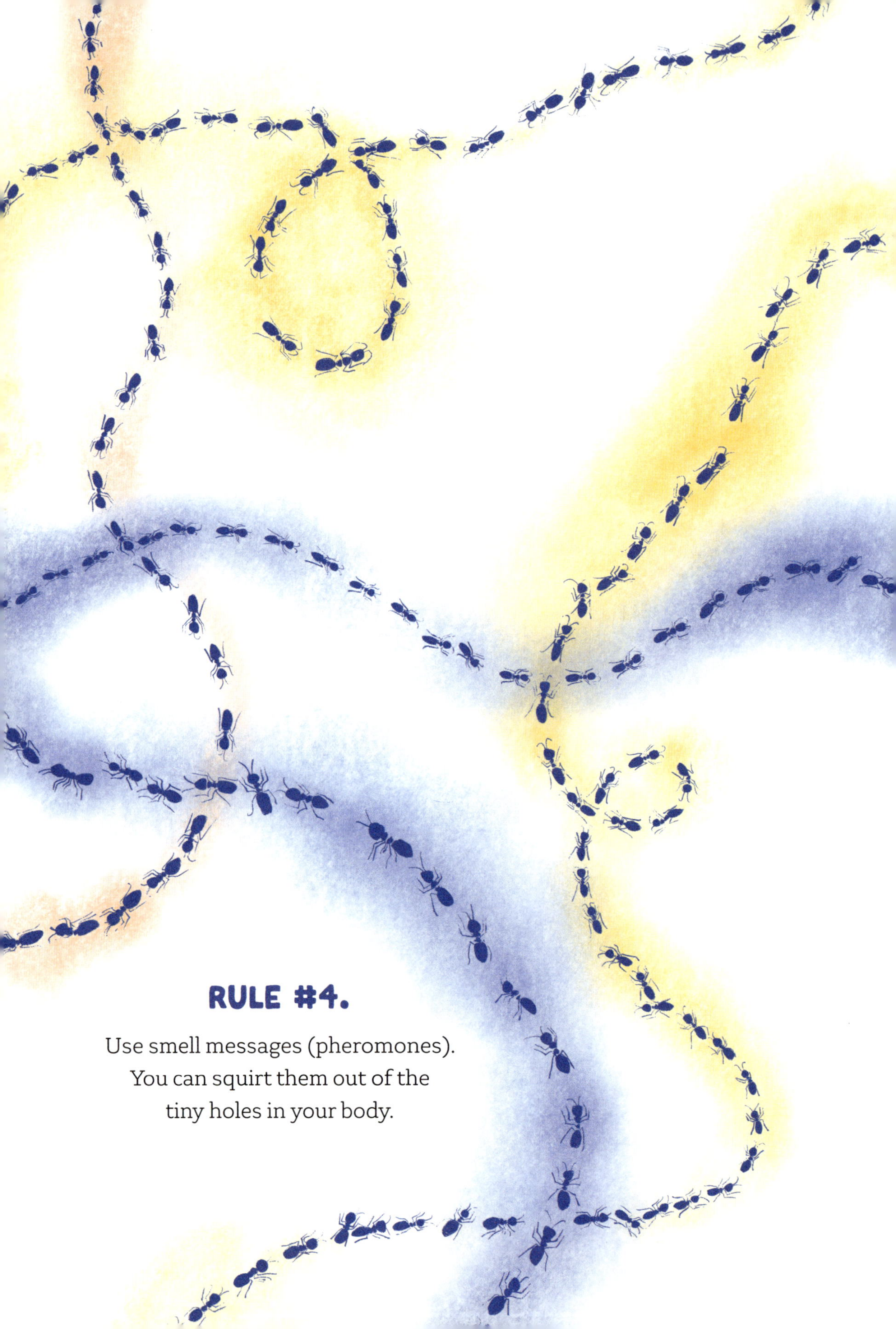

RULE #4.

Use smell messages (pheromones).
You can squirt them out of the
tiny holes in your body.

You can smell pheromones with your antennae.

GOOD FOR: Drawing paths, saying 'follow me', telling others about cool stuff you've found.

Most importantly, remember to wear our colony's secret signature smell. We have WAY too many sisters to remember—hundreds or thousands or millions—so we need our secret signature smell to recognise each other. (See Rule #5.)

PARFUMERIE

RULE #5.

NO VISITORS ALLOWED.

Visitors might:

Make a mess (bad).

Eat our food (bad).

Eat the queen
(terrible).

Eat you
(bad).

Smell the ants around you.
Do they smell like our
secret signature smell?

Yes: OK.
No: Kick them out.

DEPARTMENT OF ANTS
SIGNATURE SMELL
TEAM SPIRIT
6 LEGS
2 ANTENNAE
QUEEN

RULE #6.

Share your food. Bring it back to the nest. Put some in your crop (the pocket in your throat, before your stomach) then spit it back up for others to eat.

Or ooze it out through the tiny holes in your body
so that your sisters can lick it off you later.

RULE #7A.

Be nice to your baby sisters (and the occasional brother). Bring them food when they're hungry. Use your tongue to keep them clean.

Yes, even if they're tiny, or squirmy, or if they don't do anything except lie there inside their cocoons being boring*.

* Boring on the outside. There's actually a lot going on in there.

Remember, you used to be an egg (then a larva, then a pupa) too.

RULE #7B.

AN EGG IS NOT
A FOOTBALL.

It is also not:

A chair.

Breakfast.

A present.

A wig holder.

A good skater.

RULE #8.

Keep the nest tidy. Move rubbish to the bin pile, or outside. DO NOT leave poo, dead ants, etc. in shared living spaces. It's unhygienic.

RECYCLE
DONATE

RULE #9.
If you see something dangerous, spray the ALARM SMELL and make the ALARM NOISE.
If you smell the alarm smell or hear the alarm noise, help.

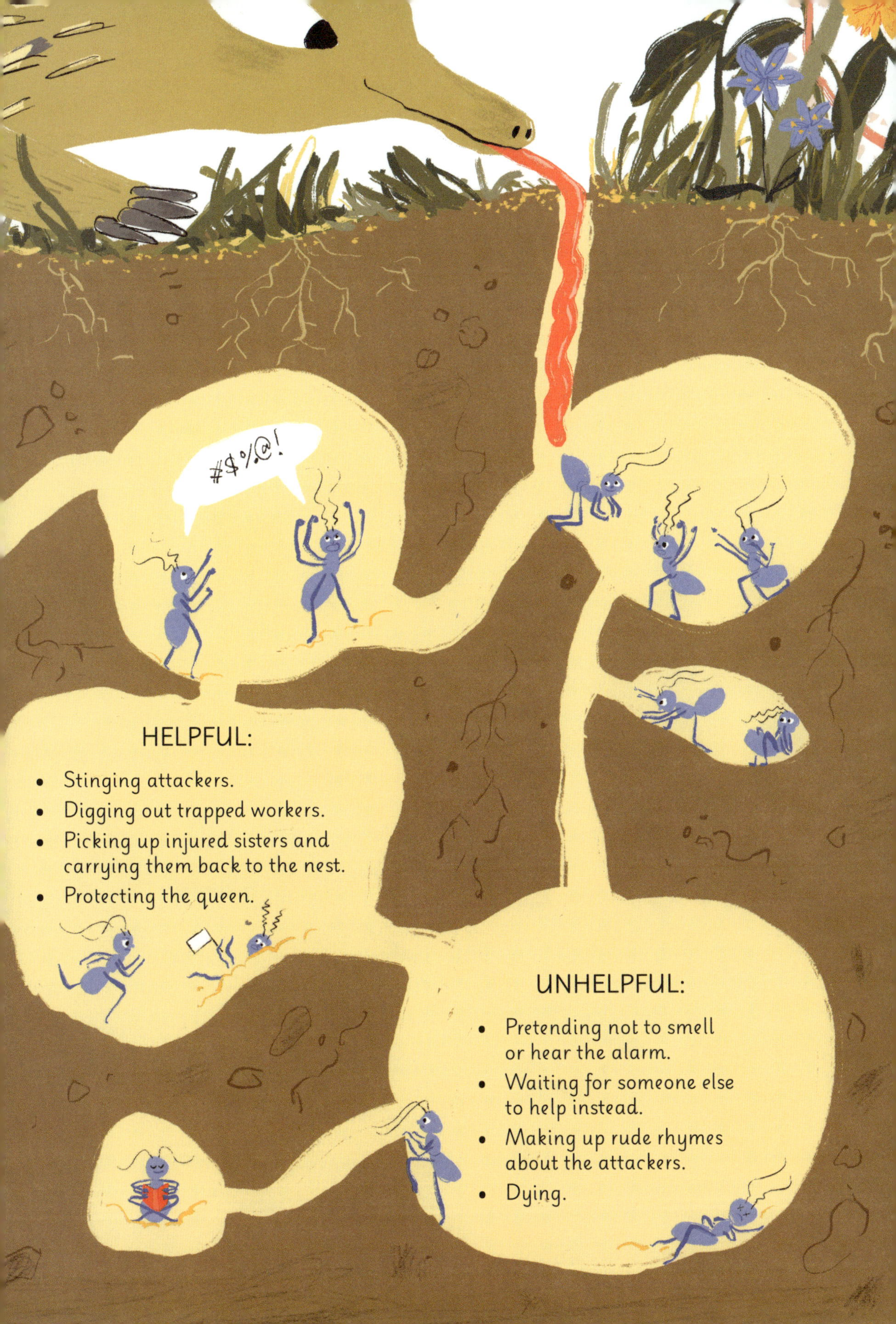

HELPFUL:

- Stinging attackers.
- Digging out trapped workers.
- Picking up injured sisters and carrying them back to the nest.
- Protecting the queen.

UNHELPFUL:

- Pretending not to smell or hear the alarm.
- Waiting for someone else to help instead.
- Making up rude rhymes about the attackers.
- Dying.

RULE #10.

Watch out for humans. They are sometimes mean to ants because they don't like sharing their homes and food. (They don't understand that we are just following the ant rules.)

NOTE: Consider writing ant rules book for humans.

RULE #11.

Follow all the rules. They help our colony to work together, look after each other, survive, and grow.

If we all follow the ant rules,
we can achieve anything ...

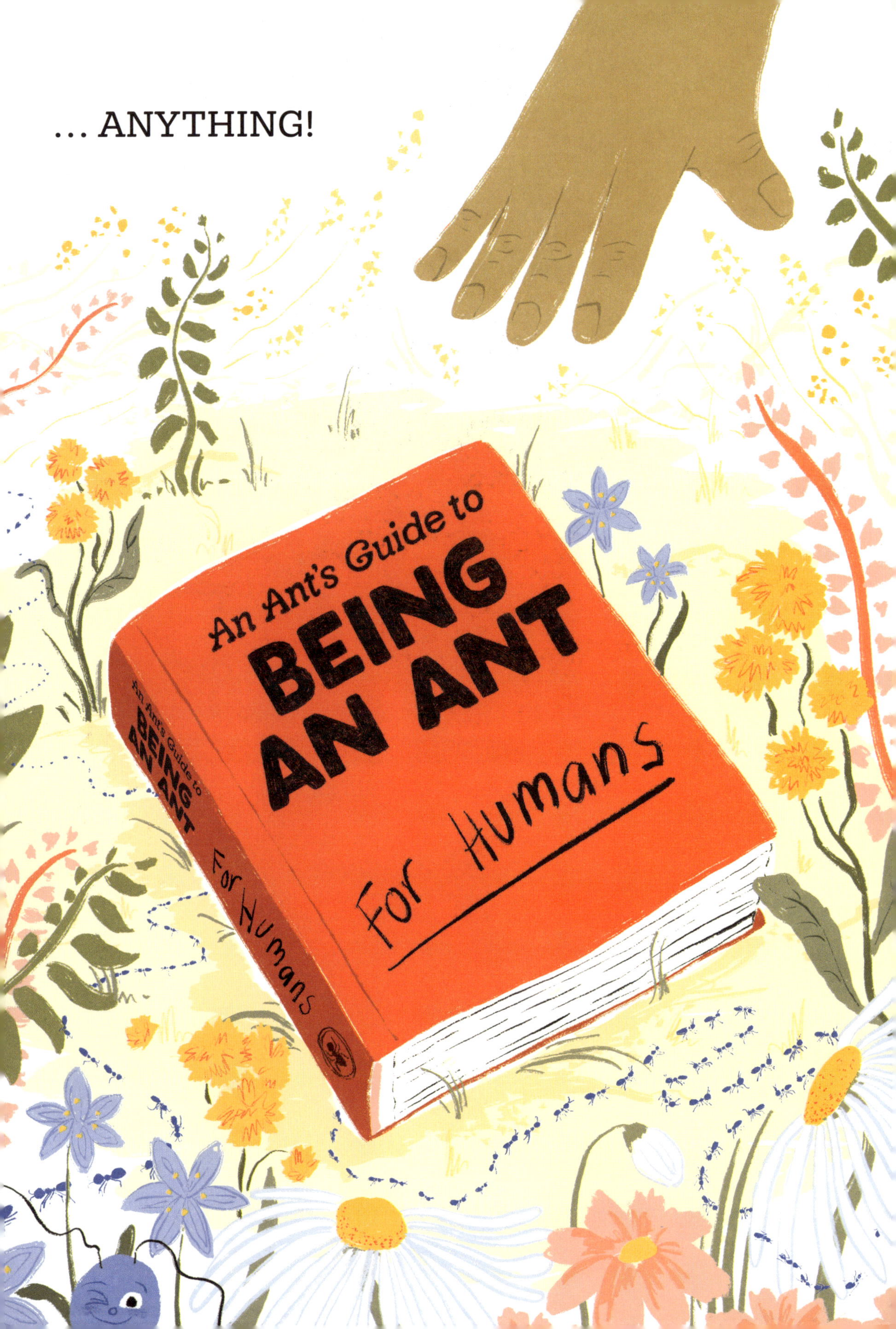
... ANYTHING!
An Ant's Guide to
BEING AN ANT
For Humans
An Ant's Guide to
BEING AN ANT
For Humans

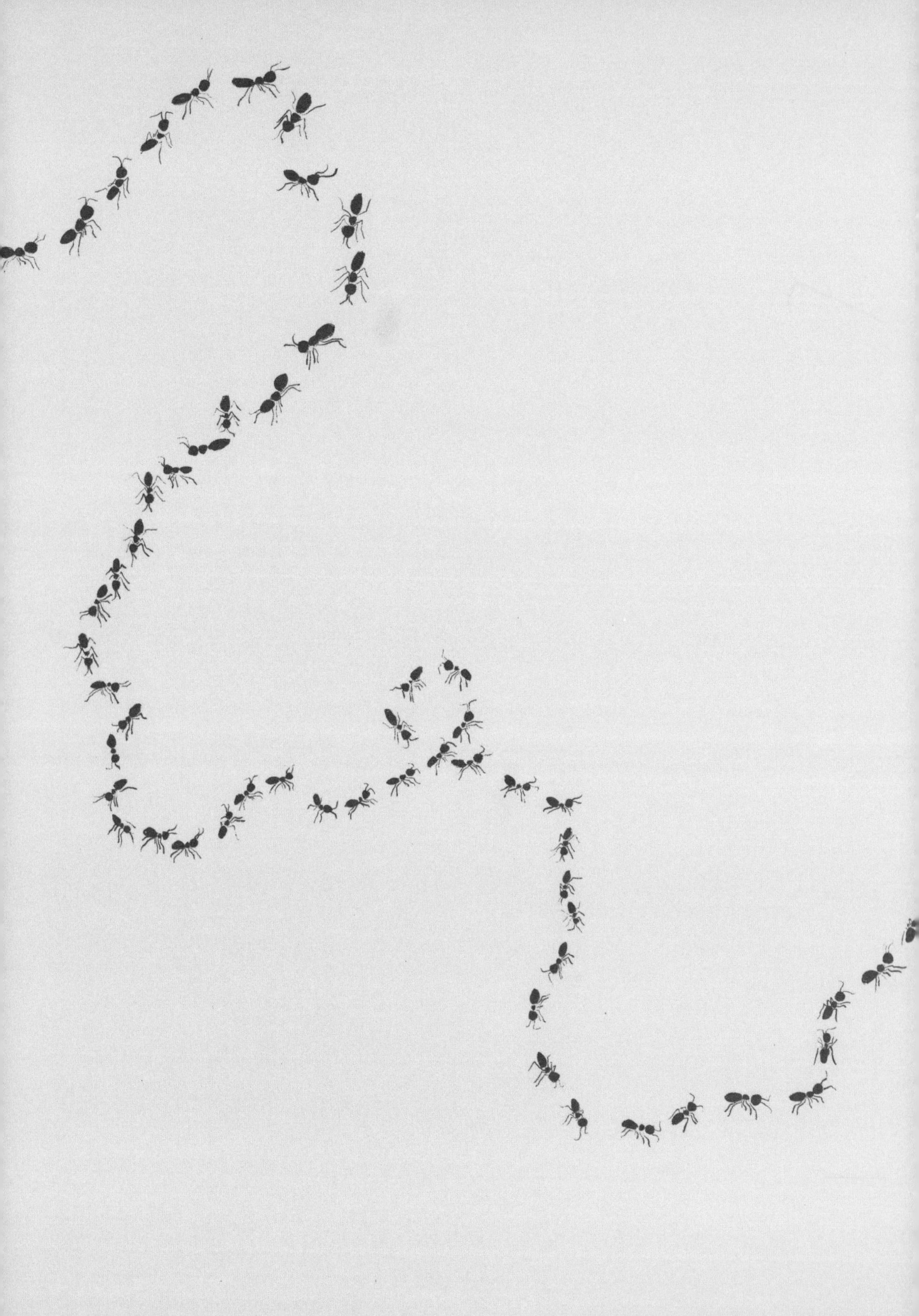